NATIONAL HOCKEY LEAGUE

BY DAVID RAUSCH

EPIC

BELLWETHER MEDIA • MINNEAPOLIS, MN

EPIC

EPIC BOOKS are no ordinary books. They burst with intense action, high-speed heroics, and shadows of the unknown. Are you ready for an Epic adventure?

This edition first published in 2015 by Bellwether Media, Inc.

Library of Congress Cataloging-in-Publication Data

Rausch, David.
National Hockey League / by David Rausch.
pages cm. – (Epic : Major League Sports)
Includes bibliographical references and index.
Summary: "Engaging images accompany information about the National Hockey League. The combination of high-interest subject matter and light text is intended for students in grades 2 through 7"– Provided by publisher.
ISBN 978-1-62617-137-4 (hardcover : alk. paper)
1. National Hockey League–Juvenile literature. 2. Hockey–Juvenile literature. I. Title.
GV847.8.N3R38 2014
796.962'64–dc23

2014014025

Printed in the United States of America, North Mankato, MN.

TABLE OF CONTENTS

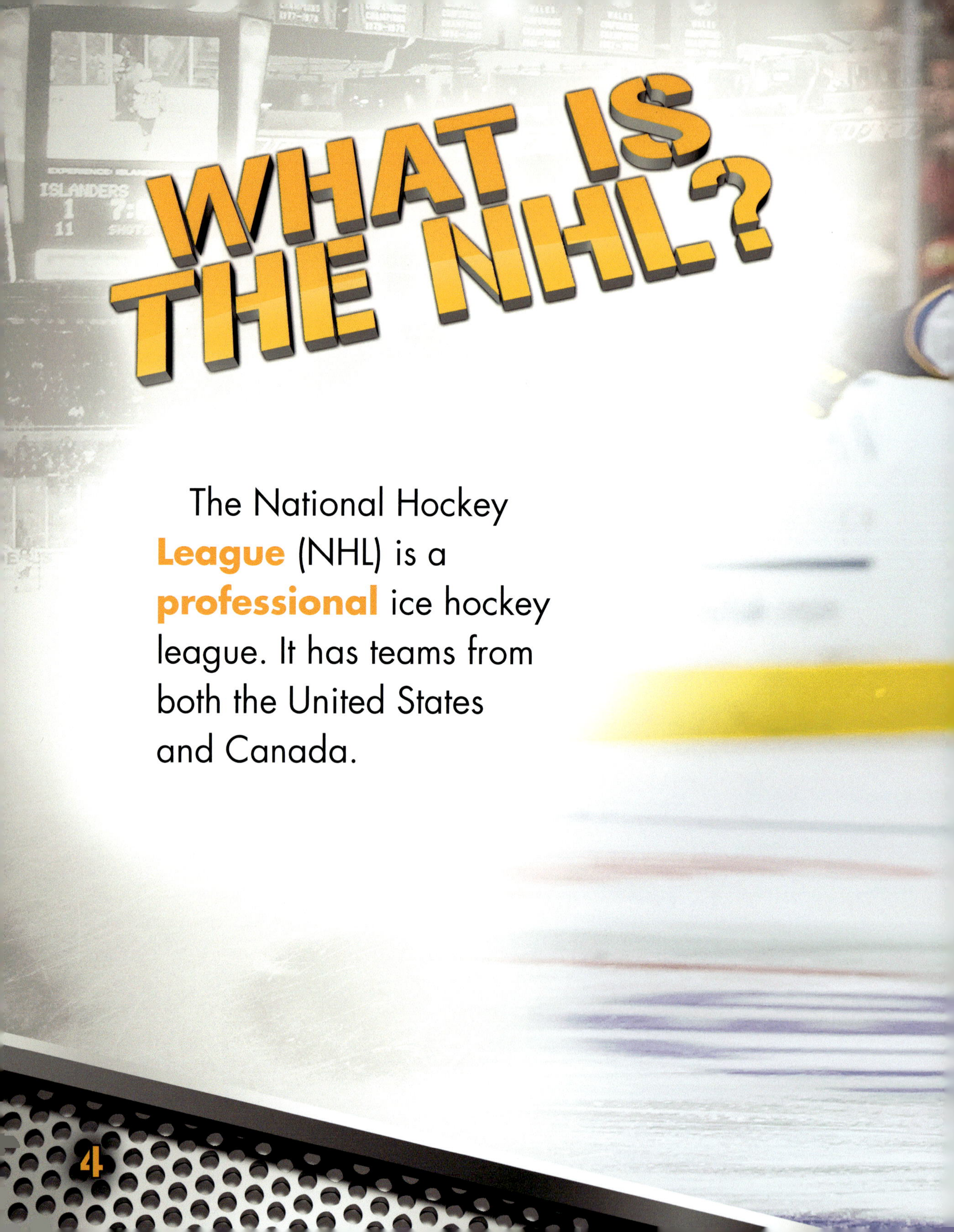

WHAT IS THE NHL?

The National Hockey **League** (NHL) is a **professional** ice hockey league. It has teams from both the United States and Canada.

88
BAUER
74

HISTORY OF THE NHL

The International Pro Hockey League (IPHL) was the first pro league. It lasted from 1904 until 1907. Then the National Hockey Association (NHA) formed in 1909.

THE PCHA

The Pacific Coast Hockey Association (PCHA) was another pro league from 1911 to 1924. It was the first league to add blue lines to the ice and numbers to players' sweaters. Forward passes were also allowed.

Vancouver Millionaires
of the PCHA (1913)

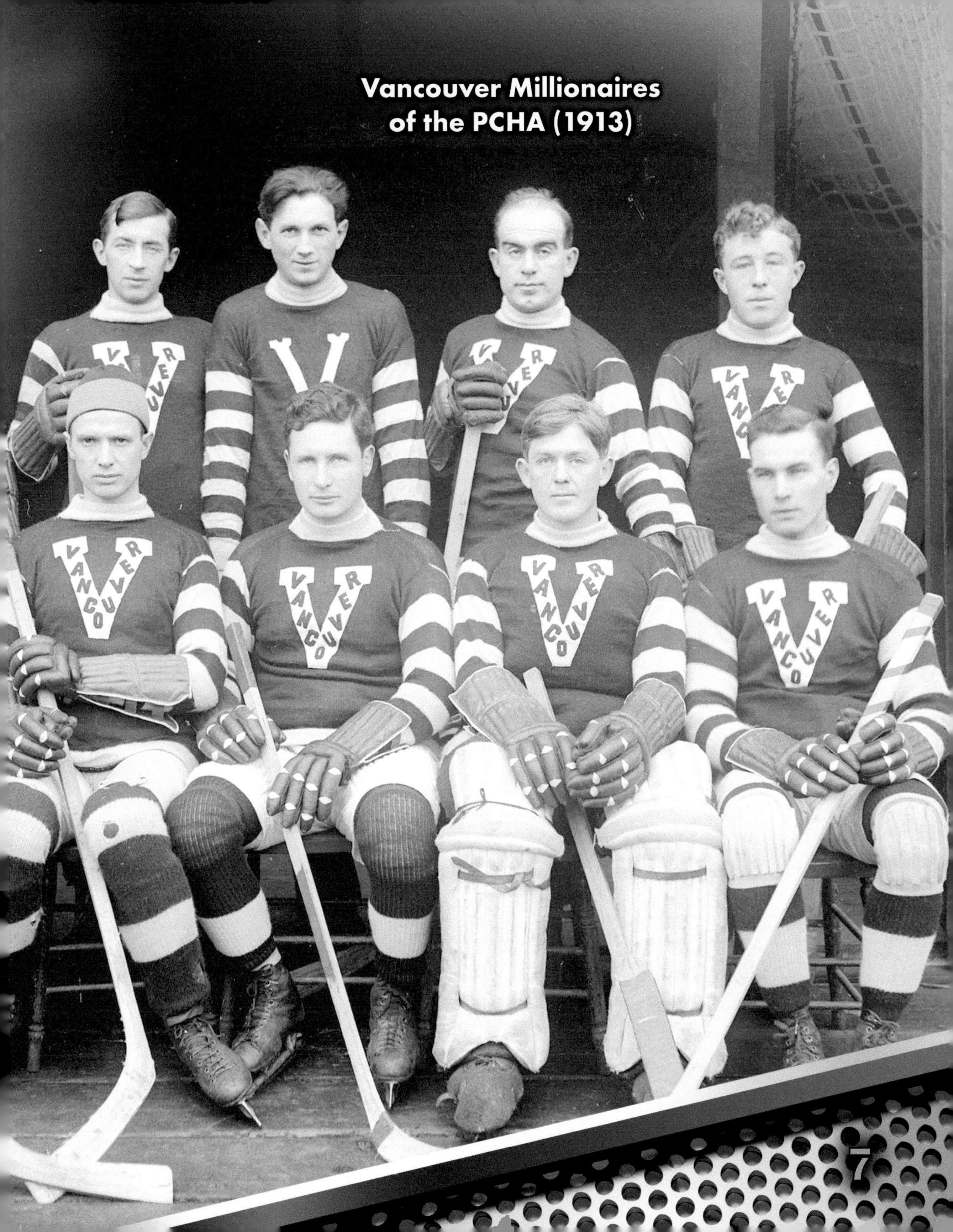

In 1917, four teams left the NHA. They and a new Toronto team started a new league. This was the beginning of the NHL.

A LOOK BACK

1904:	The International Professional Hockey League forms.
December 7, 1911:	The Pacific Coast Hockey Association forms.
November 26, 1917:	Five hockey teams create the National Hockey League.
March 30, 1918:	The Toronto Arenas are the first NHL team to win the Stanley Cup. They defeat the Vancouver Millionaires, the PCHA champions.
February 14, 1934:	The Toronto Maple Leafs play a team of all-stars. This first All-Star Game raises money for injured player Ace Bailey.
February 25, 1940:	An NHL game is shown on television for the first time in the U.S.
March 10, 1955:	A Zamboni machine cleans NHL ice for the first time.
August 26, 1961:	The Hockey Hall of Fame opens in Toronto, Ontario.
June 5, 1963:	The NHL has its first draft of young players. The first player picked is Garry Monahan.
February 6, 2000:	The NHL retires Wayne Gretzky's sweater number, 99. He held 61 league records when he retired the year before.

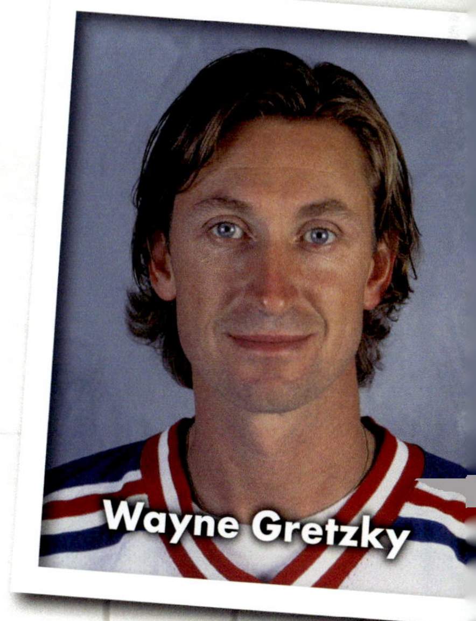
Wayne Gretzky

THE TEAMS

The NHL has 30 teams. There are 16 teams in the Eastern **Conference** and 14 teams in the Western Conference. Each conference has two **divisions**.

EASTERN CONFERENCE

Atlantic Division

- Boston Bruins
- Buffalo Sabres
- Detroit Red Wings
- Florida Panthers
- Montreal Canadiens
- Ottawa Senators
- Tampa Bay Lightning
- Toronto Maple Leafs

Metropolitan Division

- Carolina Hurricanes
- Columbus Blue Jackets
- New Jersey Devils
- New York Islanders
- New York Rangers
- Philadelphia Flyers
- Pittsburgh Penguins
- Washington Capitals

WESTERN CONFERENCE

Central Division

- Chicago Blackhawks
- Colorado Avalanche
- Dallas Stars
- Minnesota Wild
- Nashville Predators
- St. Louis Blues
- Winnipeg Jets

Pacific Division

- Anaheim Ducks
- Calgary Flames
- Edmonton Oilers
- Los Angeles Kings
- Phoenix Coyotes
- San Jose Sharks
- Vancouver Canucks

RANGERS

Each team's **active roster** has 18 **skaters** and 2 goalies. Teams add young players through the NHL **draft**. They also trade players and sign **free agents**.

NHL draft

PLAYING THE GAME

Every game has three 20-minute **periods**. A **face-off** starts each period. **Referees** call penalties when players break the rules. The team with the most goals wins.

TIE GAME

A tie game goes into overtime. This period lasts five minutes. A shootout happens if neither team scores.

HOCKEY TALK

assist—when a player passes the puck to another player who scores a goal; a goal can have one or two assists.

body check—when a player hits an opponent with his hip or shoulder; the opponent must have the puck or had it last.

deke—when a player with the puck fakes out an opponent

goal—when a player hits the puck into the opponent's net; 1 point

hat trick—when a player scores three goals in one game

penalty—when a player breaks a rule and has to sit in the penalty box for a period of time

power play—when one team has more players on the ice than their opponent; power plays happen when players go to the penalty box.

save—when the goalie blocks a shot that would have been a goal

shootout—when three players from each team take turns shooting against a goalie; shootouts take place if teams are still tied after overtime.

slap shot—when the puck is hit with a full backswing

THE REGULAR SEASON

Each team has training camp in September. They also play preseason games to prepare. The regular season begins in October. It is 82 games long.

THE PLAYOFFS AND THE STANLEY CUP FINALS

Each division's three best teams make the playoffs. Each conference also has two **wildcard** teams. Teams play until each conference has a champion.

56
CCM
MINNESOTA WILD
Reebok
28
Smith

The conference champions face off in the Stanley Cup Finals. The winning team gets its players' names added to the Stanley Cup trophy!

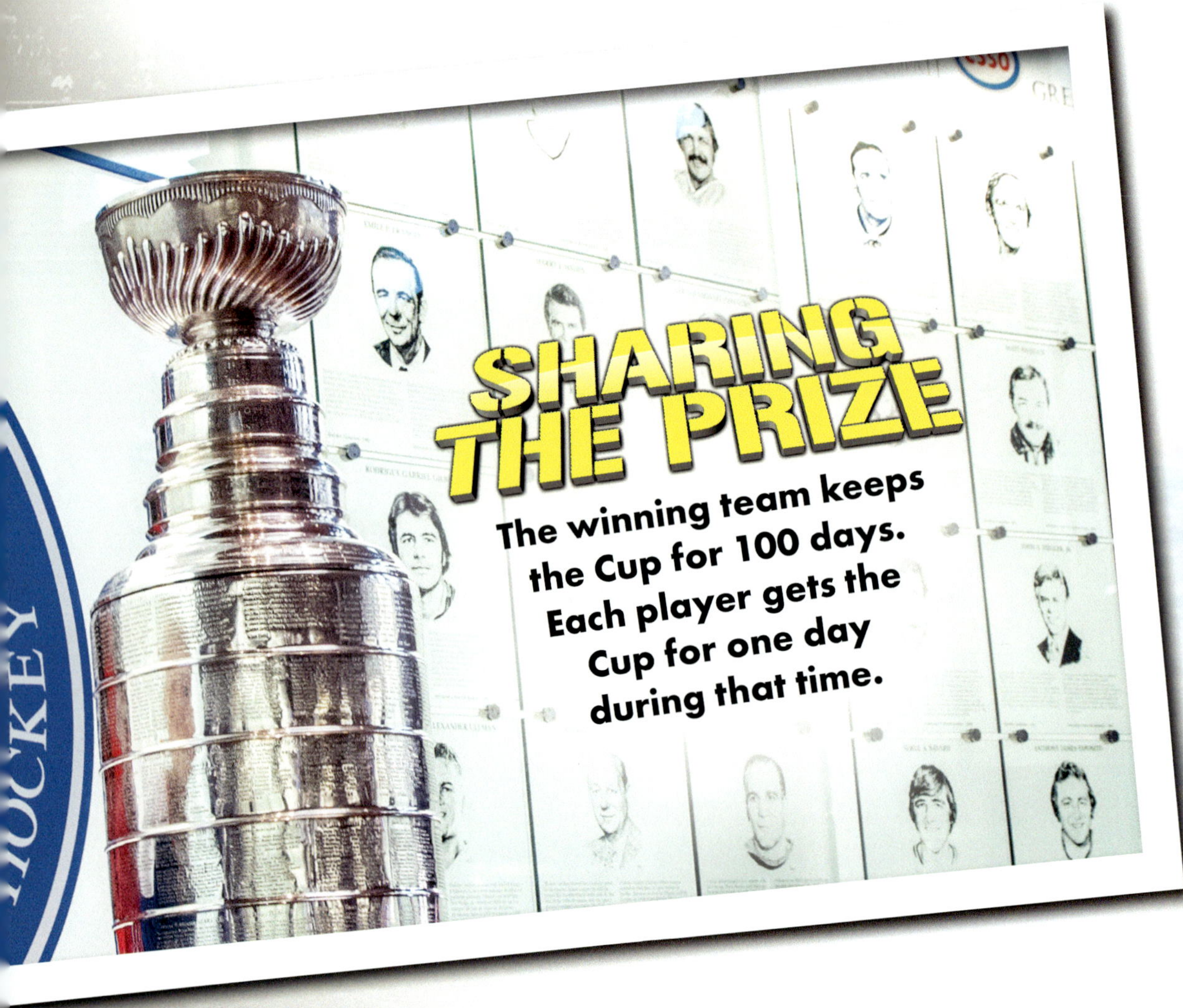

SHARING THE PRIZE

The winning team keeps the Cup for 100 days. Each player gets the Cup for one day during that time.

WARRIOR
VAUGHN
32
LA
VAUGHN
ZUCCARELLO
Reebok

GLOSSARY

active roster—a list of players on a team who can play in an NHL game

conference—a group of sports teams within a league; teams in a conference often play one another.

divisions—groups of sports teams within a conference; teams in a division often play one another.

draft—a yearly event in which NHL teams pick young players to play for them

face-off—the action that begins play in a hockey game; a referee drops the puck between two players from opposing teams.

free agents—professional athletes who are free to play for any team; free agents do not have contracts.

league—a group of people or teams united by a common interest or activity

periods—the three divisions of time in a hockey game

professional—at a level where athletes get paid to play a sport

referees—people who enforce the rules during a game

skaters—players who move around the ice to play offense or defense

wildcard—a team that makes the playoffs without winning the division

TO LEARN MORE

At the Library

Frederick, Shane. *The Best of Everything Hockey Book*. Mankato, Minn.: Capstone Press, 2011.

Jordan, Christopher. *We Are the Goal Scorers: The Top Point Leaders of the NHL*. New York, N.Y.: Fenn/Tundra, 2013.

Peters, Chris. *The Stanley Cup Finals*. Minneapolis, Minn.: ABDO Pub. Co., 2013.

On the Web

Learning more about the National Hockey League is as easy as 1, 2, 3.

1. Go to www.factsurfer.com.

2. Enter "National Hockey League" into the search box.

3. Click the "Surf" button and you will see a list of related web sites.

With factsurfer.com, finding more information is just a click away.

INDEX

The images in this book are reproduced through the courtesy of: Robin Alam/ Icon SMI/ Corbis, front cover (left), pp. 4-5; Michael Tureski/ Icon SMI/ Corbis, front cover (right); Library and Archives Canada, pp. 6-7, 8; NHL/ KRT/ Newscom, p. 9; Mark Goldman/ Icon SMI/ Corbis, p. 10; Jeanine Leech/ Icon SMI/ Corbis, p. 12; Bill Kostroun/ AP/ Corbis, p. 13; Chris Seward/ MCT/ Newscom, p. 14; SMI/ Newscom, pp. 16-17, 21; Mike Wulf/ Cal Sport Media/ Newscom, p. 19; Rick D'Elia/ Corbis, p. 20.